BEST *in* SHOW

24 Appliqué Quilts for Dog Lovers

CAROL ARMSTRONG

Text copyright © 2009 by Carol Armstrong

Artwork copyright © 2009 by C&T Publishing, Inc.

Publisher: Amy Marson

Creative Director: Gailen Runge

Editors: Jake Finch and Stacy Chamness

Technical Editors: Wendy Mathson and Ann Haley

Copyeditor/Proofreader: Wordfirm Inc.

Cover Designer: Kristy K. Zacharias

Book Designer: Aliza Shalit

Production Coordinator: Kirstie L. Pettersen

Illustrator: Wendy Mathson

Photography by Christina Carty-Francis and Diane Pedersen of C&T Publishing, Inc., unless otherwise noted

Published by C&T Publishing, Inc., P.O. Box 1456, Lafayette, CA 94549

Library of Congress Cataloging-in-Publication Data

Armstrong, Carol

  Best in show--24 appliqué quilts for dog lovers / Carol Armstrong.

    p. cm.

  Summary: "22 favorite dog breeds are represented in 24 charming little appliqué portrait quilts that practically sit up and say woof"--Provided by publisher.

  ISBN 978-1-57120-610-7 (paper trade : alk. paper)

  1. Appliqué--Patterns. 2. Quilting. 3. Dogs in art. I. Title. II. Title: Appliqué quilts for dog lovers.

  TT779.A75798 2009

  746.44'5--dc22

                    2008043647

Printed in China

10 9 8 7 6 5 4 3 2 1

ntents

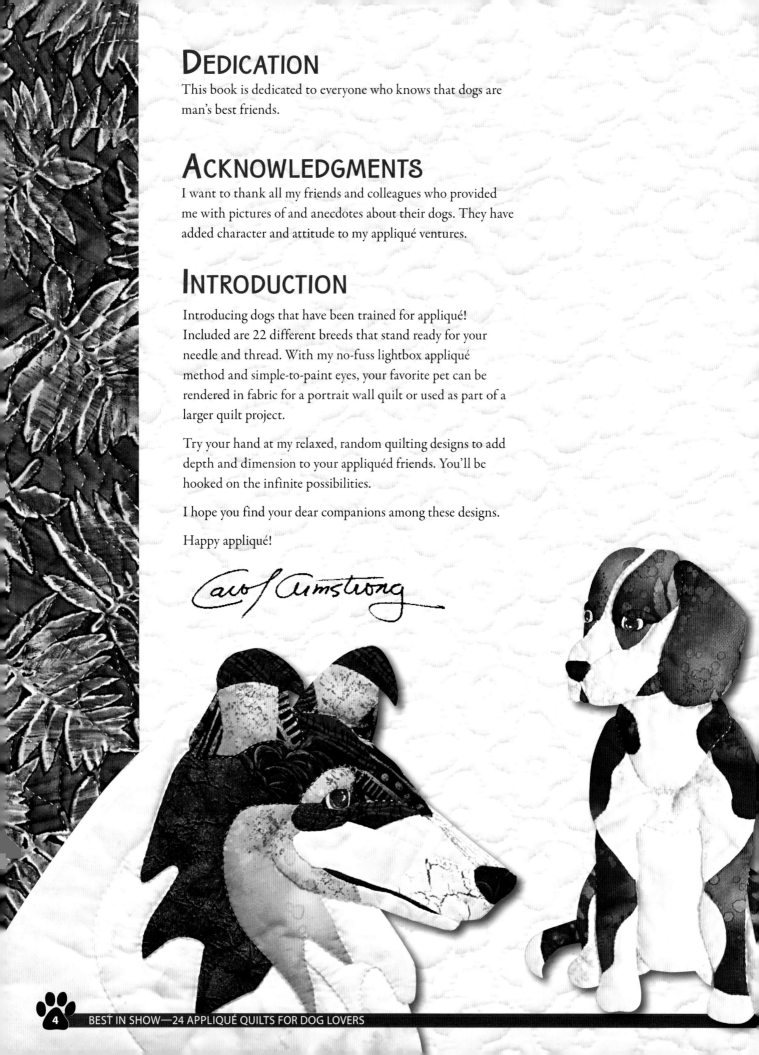

DEDICATION

This book is dedicated to everyone who knows that dogs are man's best friends.

ACKNOWLEDGMENTS

I want to thank all my friends and colleagues who provided me with pictures of and anecdotes about their dogs. They have added character and attitude to my appliqué ventures.

INTRODUCTION

Introducing dogs that have been trained for appliqué! Included are 22 different breeds that stand ready for your needle and thread. With my no-fuss lightbox appliqué method and simple-to-paint eyes, your favorite pet can be rendered in fabric for a portrait wall quilt or used as part of a larger quilt project.

Try your hand at my relaxed, random quilting designs to add depth and dimension to your appliquéd friends. You'll be hooked on the infinite possibilities.

I hope you find your dear companions among these designs.

Happy appliqué!

Carol Armstrong

Chapter 1

SUPPLIES

TOOLS

Having the right supplies and materials at the ready makes any project easier to construct. Here are the basics.

Lightbox My method of appliqué uses tracing as a vital element. A good lightbox is handy and will be useful for other craft pursuits beyond appliqué. In lieu of a lightbox, a window on a bright day, or a glass table lit from below with a low-wattage bulb, will suffice.

Needles, Pins, and Thimbles For appliqué, I use a size 10 or 11 straw or milliner's needle; the longer length helps in turning stitches. For quilting, I use a size 8, 9, or 10 sharps. This works well for quilting without a frame, which is my preferred method. Short ¾″ pins with rounded heads are great for appliqué. Thimbles are quite a personal fit. While quilting, I use a leather thimble on the pushing finger. Check out your favorite quilting shop for a selection of options.

Cutting Tools A rotary cutter, a mat, and a selection of rulers are great for cutting borders and binding and squaring backgrounds after the appliqué is finished. Sharp scissors that snip right down to the tip are a must. Have both large and small on hand.

Marking Tools Water-removable marking pens are needed for lightbox appliqué. I use a blue or white pen, depending on the fabric color. The markings can be removed with a wet paper towel. Always allow the fabric to air dry after removing the marker. Read and follow the directions for your brand. And, of course, be sure to test the markers and do not iron the marks.

Iron A good steam iron is a must for pressing seams and appliqué. I press appliqué from the back on a soft surface, such as a folded white towel.

MATERIALS

Threads I use a cotton-wrapped polyester thread for appliqué. To match the color, place a single strand of thread on the fabric for comparison. Match your appliqué thread to the appliqué fabric as closely as you can.

The best thread for quilting is a thread specifically made for quilting. Some threads are for handwork and others are for machine sewing; usually their use is clearly

marked. I used natural-color thread for all the quilting in this book, but do not hesitate to try your hand at using the rest of the rainbow.

Embroidery floss can be used for some details if you like. In a few pieces, I used floss for the outlines. Generally, I use two strands of floss and a stem stitch (page 17).

Fabric Start with a small selection to make your first project. Then, as your quilting skills grow, you'll add more colors to your stash. Of course you will never have all the fabric you need for a project because, as we know, there is always one more that is a must-have. Your local quilt shop will be happy to help you in selecting fabrics for that special quilt.

I use a wide variety of prints for fur. The first criterion in choosing the fabric is the print's color; the second is the print's texture. Tone-on-tone prints are fabulous. Simple, quiet prints work best. A busy print will hide the lines between the appliqué pieces, which are an important part of the overall design. Don't forget to audition the back of some prints. Quite often this will help you find the same color in a lighter or darker value. For example, in the Magyar Vizsla on page 44, the eyebrows are made from the reverse of the fabric used on the top of the muzzle.

Your choice of breed will help dictate the colors you choose for the dog's body. I cut out the entire appliqué motif to audition my fabric choices. This is the best time to make changes.

For the backgrounds, I use a good-quality, unbleached muslin. A light color also works, but to keep the quilting highlighted, avoid prints unless they are very subtle.

As far as the borders go, the sky's the limit. The same goes for the binding. I try to pull some of the colors from the dog into the border print, such as the gold from the Golden Retriever on page 39 or the rusty brown from the Beagle on page 26. Or I select fabrics that will complement the dog's colors, such as the blue for the West Highland White Terrier on page 55 or the pink for the Pug on page 49. Using a fun print, such as the Scottie dog print for the Scottish Terrier on page 51, is another option.

The more designs you appliqué, the better your color instincts will become. I still make several changes from my original fabric picks on most projects.

Batting For good dimension and quilting definition, a needle-punched polyester batting is my favorite. A thin, all-cotton batting is nice but gives less shadow to the overall quilting design. Make a couple of samples using different battings to choose your own favorite.

Eye Materials The eyes on the dogs are painted on muslin, cut out, and glued in place. This gives you infinite control over the dogs' expressions.

  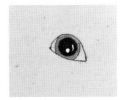

Supplies for painting eyes:

- 🐾 Muslin

- 🐾 Freezer paper (optional)

- 🐾 Tube acrylic, fabric, or craft paints
  (colors of paint used: blue, white, black, iridescent gold, rust, pink)

- 🐾 Tiny paintbrush

- 🐾 Black paint pen (I use a Setaskrib+; a Pigma pen will also work.)

- 🐾 Toothpick

- 🐾 Fabric glue

- 🐾 Acrylic gloss varnish (optional)

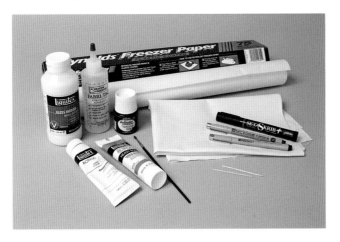

Embellishments The quilts in this book are simple portraits of faithful friends. You can add some fun embellishments to your pet's portrait. A ribbon collar with a heart pendant and a fabric flower adorn the Bichon Frise on page 28. The Labrador Retriever sits on a plaid footstool on page 42, but you could change it to a stone wall, a dog bed, or a grassy hill. Attach a dog tag or a small dog collar. Add whimsical buttons in the border or some tiny pet chew toys. Have fun and make the portrait reflect your dog's personality.

Chapter 2:

LIGHTBOX APPLIQUÉ BASICS

A lightbox gets you started working on your appliqué project quickly. No need for templates, clear overlays, or extra preparation of the appliqué pieces.

Preparing the Appliqué

1. Using a black marker, draw or trace the appliqué pattern onto plain white paper.

2. Place the traced pattern on the lightbox and secure it with a few pieces of masking tape.

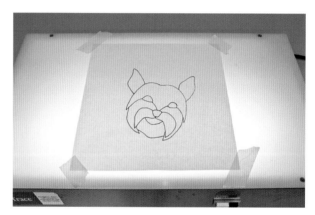

Place the dog pattern on the lightbox and tape it down.

3. Lay the fabric chosen for the background piece right side up on the pattern. Use a removable marker to trace the entire design. These lines will guide you in placing the appliqué pieces.

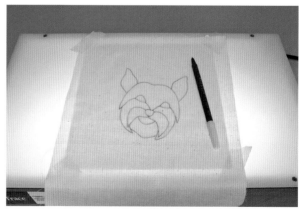

Lay the fabric over the pattern and use a removable marker to trace the pattern lines.

4. Now trace around the outer edge of each individual appliqué piece. To do this, lay the chosen fabric right side up on the pattern. Using a removable marker, trace the exact line all the way around each piece. This line will be your turn-under guideline, and it will help in the placement of successive pieces.

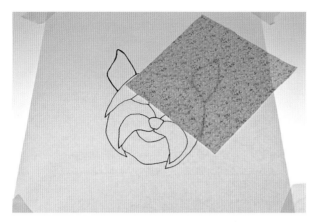

Trace the line onto the fabric to be used for each individual appliqué piece.

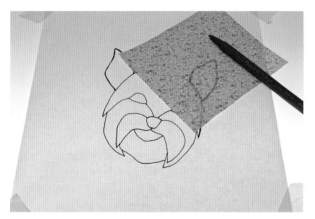

This line will be your turn-under guideline.

5. Cut out each piece ³⁄₁₆″ to ¼″ outside the line. Don't skimp on the turn-under allowance. You can always trim it away later if it is in the way.

Cut out the appliqué piece, leaving a generous turn-under allowance around it. You can always trim it later.

TIP

Cheap, thin copy paper lets the light through more easily than the good stuff does.

TIP

If you can't see through the fabric to trace the pattern, go over the pattern's black lines with a red marker. I use a red Sharpie. It shows through dark brown, green, and black fabrics. Take the pattern off the lightbox **first**, as the red marker may bleed through the paper.

Order of Appliqué When you appliqué, begin with the pieces that are farthest and then work forward (that is, from background to foreground). I have numbered the appliqué patterns to indicate the order of appliqué. As you gain more experience, the order will become more evident.

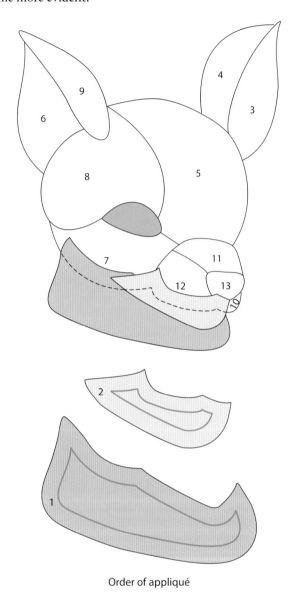

Order of appliqué

> ## TIP
>
> Mark the number of the piece on the turn-under allowance. This is handy when many pieces are similar in shape and color.

Stitching Important: Only stitch down those edges that will not be covered by another appliquéd piece. Begin with piece 1. Position it on the background using the lines on the background and the lines on the piece itself. Use a few pins to hold it in place. Try to stitch in a continuous line when you can. Using your finger or the needle, turn under the allowance as you sew. Allow your stitching to be close rather than perfect. Close is good here. The removable marker on both the piece and the background will be erased later.

Pre-appliqué Sometimes it is better to appliqué two or more pieces together before applying them to the background. This is especially effective where two pieces of appliqué meet along a continuous line. Pre-appliqué creates a smooth turn-under line. I have noted on the patterns where this technique is useful.

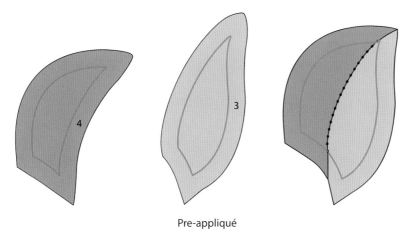

Pre-appliqué

The appliqué order usually remains the same, as does curve snipping (page 14) and the appliqué stitch. The rule to remember is: Do not stitch the piece together in the turn-under allowance. Leaving it loose allows the fabric free to turn as a clip would. Change the color of thread while sewing around the completed multipiece appliqué as the fabric changes.

The Stitch

1. Place the piece to be appliquéd in position on the background. Use a few pins if necessary to hold the pieces in place. Whenever possible, begin stitching at a place on the appliqué shape that will give you a continuous line.

2. Thread a size 10 or 11 milliner's or straw needle with a single strand of thread about 12″ to 18″ long. Any longer and your strand of thread will fray before you use it all. Knot the thread. Turn under the allowance up to the marked line. Slip the knot into the fold of the turn-under by running the needle through the fold from the back of the piece and out onto the edge to be stitched down. This hides the knot in the fold.

The knot is hidden within the turn-under allowance's fold.

![TIP ribbon] TIP

To turn under the allowance with your needle, prick the allowance with the tip of the needle and push the allowance sideways and under. Trust me—it becomes easier after some practice.

Use the tip of the needle to pick up and push under the allowance.

3. To avoid pushing the background fabric as you needle-turn, keep the background fabric somewhat taut as you work. I sew with the piece on my leg. You can use a small pillow on your lap too. The friction of the background fabric on my jeans is sufficient to hold it well. If you are stitching near the edge of the background, it is helpful to pin the background fabric to your jeans or the pillow to offer some resistance. You will have to turn and re-pin as you stitch the piece.

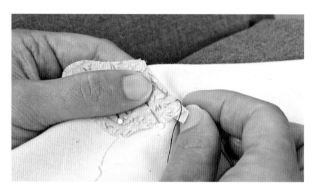

Holding the appliqué on your legs can help keep the fabric taut.

4. Insert the needle into the background at a point that is even with the thread's exit from the appliqué piece.

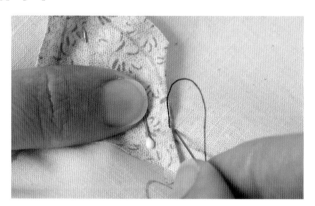

Insert the needle into the background.

5. With the needle still under the background, move the needle tip forward.

6. Come up through the background and through a few threads on the folded edge of the appliqué piece. Pull the thread snug without drawing up the fabric.

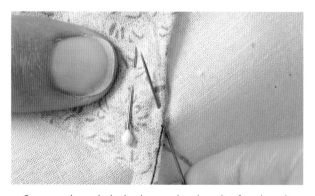

Come up through the background and catch a few threads on the folded edge of the appliqué piece.

7. Insert the needle into the background again, so it is even with the thread's exit from the appliqué piece, and continue with another stitch.

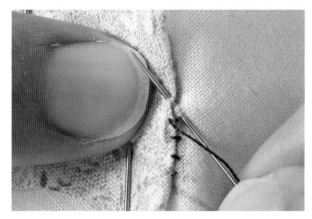

Repeat the steps to make the next stitch.

8. Turn your work as you sew to keep the stitches even and your wrist straight. Stitch away from yourself, or from right to left for right-handed sewers and from left to right for left-handers, like me. With a bit of practice, your stitches will become small, even, and easy.

If you turn the appliqué work over to the back, this is what the stitches will look like.

9. To end the stitching of your appliqué piece, take 3 stitches in the same place, either from the front, where the stitches will be covered by the next appliqué piece, or from the back behind an appliqué piece, through just the background fabric. Clip the thread.

Work on keeping your stitch size consistent and your turn-under smooth. Allow yourself some imperfections. Many will disappear with pressing. Enjoy the process.

Pressing Pressing your appliqué works wonders to finish your piece. It smoothes out little bumps, sinks the stitches into hiding, and flattens the background. Press your appliqué with some steam on a cushioned board after removing any markings. I use a folded white towel for extra padding. Wiggle your iron across the back of the piece to avoid creating wrinkles.

SPECIAL TURNS

Outside curves Turn under a little bit of the piece's fabric edge at a time to keep the edge smooth. Note that it is easier to turn a curve when it is cut along the bias of the fabric. (Bias is 45° on the fabric in relation to the selvage.) Take more time when you are turning under fabric closer to the straight of grain. You may clip here and there if you find it helpful.

Inside curves The bias versus straight-grain rule comes into play here also. Straight of grain runs selvage to selvage or end to end. You can line up a curved shape in a bias direction, but some curves always end up off-bias. Clip the inside curves through the turn-under allowance, just shy of the marked line.

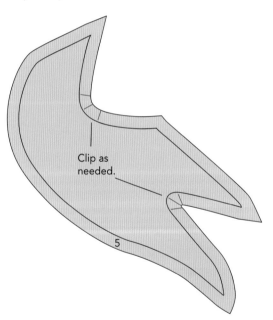

Clip as needed.

5

Clipping inside curves

On tighter inside curves, such as the Collie's neck fur on page 32, stitch up to the curve and clip into the turn-under allowance, just shy of the marked line. Keep stitching down into the curve. When the fabric becomes difficult to turn, use the needle to turn under the allowance on the far side of the clip. Hold this in place. Continue by placing the needle under the appliqué. Pivot upward into the turn-under, rolling the allowance under, and stitch in place. Adjust the turn-under as close to the reference lines as you can. Close but not perfect will work fine here. Look at the appliqué as a whole picture, not just little pieces. Practice will make this turning style easier.

Points Start out with the knowledge that not all points are equal; some points are pointier than others.

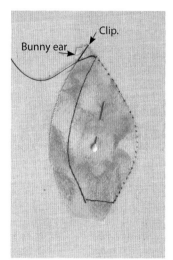 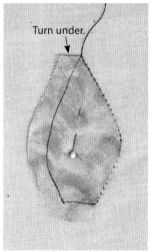 

Turning points

When you reach a point in your appliqué, stitch right up to the point. If there is a "bunny ear" of any size, clip it off. Turning the point is now a two-step process. First, use the needle to turn under the allowance at the point at right angles. Hold this in place and pull the thread to make sure you haven't pushed too much under. Then push the side allowance under, again with the needle (see tip on page 11), and continue stitching. As always, that word *practice* is the key.

Creating Dimensional Ears

I created some fun floppy ears on several of the dogs: the Pug, the Poodle, and the Jack Russell Terrier on pages 49, 47, and 40, respectively.

1. For each ear, cut 2 pieces according to the pattern shape with the right sides of the fabric together.

2. Stitch around on the stitching line, leaving an opening. (See the individual patterns.)

3. Clip the seam allowances on any curves and turn the ears right side out. Press.

4. Insert the ears into the appliqué order as indicated. Be sure to stitch through all the layers of appliqué and the background, as this will hold things securely.

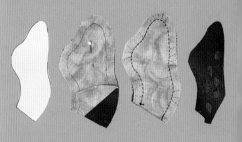

Making floppy ears

PAINTING THE EYES

Press the appliqué piece before adding the eyes. The eyes provide the spark of life for your appliquéd dog. They are all painted on muslin first, cut out, and glued in place. Some of the dogs have eye sockets, created when the appliqué is finished right up to the edge of the eye. A few eyes will be glued on top of an appliqué piece. See the individual patterns for eye placement.

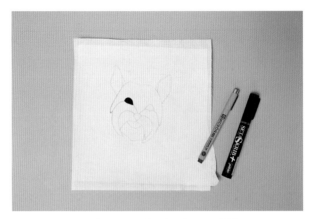

Eye socket painted on background fabric

TIP

Paint the eye socket area black or a dark color right on the background fabric, then turn under the surrounding appliqué pieces up to the painted socket edge. This is easier than painting in the socket area after the appliqué is done.

1. Trace the eyes onto a piece of muslin with a pencil or a fine Pigma pen, using the lightbox. Iron the fabric onto some freezer paper if you like to stabilize.

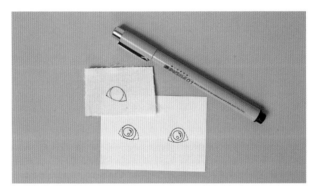

2. Using a small brush or paint pen, fill in the iris area with the desired eye color. Use the black paint pen for the pupil.

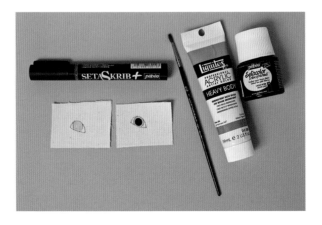

3. After the paint is dry, add a small white dot or curve to the pupil with a toothpick or a tiny brush. The location of this dot changes the dog's expression. Practicing is helpful here. The eyes are small and easy to remake if the first ones are not to your liking. I like to give the eyes a coat of acrylic gloss varnish to add some depth.

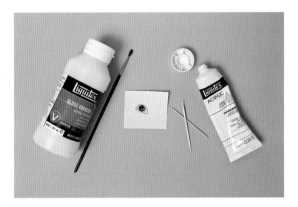

TIP

The paint prevents the cut edges of the eye from fraying.

4. After the paint is completely dry, cut out the painted area of the eye to fit the space. You may have to do some adjusting to fit the appliquéd socket, as the eyes come out slightly different each time. Glue into place with fabric glue.

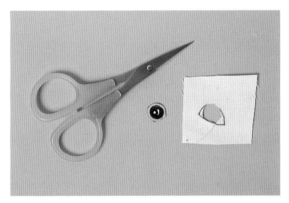

Cut out the painted eye.

EMBROIDERY

In making these dogs, I used only the stem stitch when an outline was needed, usually with 2 strands of embroidery floss.

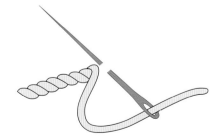

The stem stitch

Chapter 3

BORDERS, QUILTING, AND FINISHING

BORDERS

After the appliqué is complete, remove all the markings and press the piece. (See page 14.) Now, add the eyes. Using a cutting mat, rotary cutter, and ruler, trim the piece to the required size. Keep it square and remember to include ¼″ seam allowances. For those appliqué designs that touch the borders (Golden Retriever on page 39), trim the edges with the appliqué first.

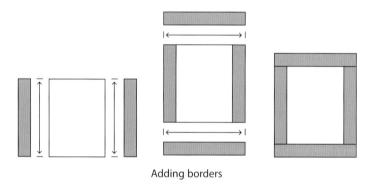

Adding borders

To add one or more borders to frame the appliqué, measure your piece to determine the correct border lengths. Using a ¼″ seam allowance, stitch on the side borders first, press, measure again, and then add the top and bottom borders.

LAYERING AND BASTING

Cut the backing and batting 1″ larger (or more) than the quilt top on all sides. Lay the backing, right side down, on your basting surface. Place the batting on top of the backing. Then add the quilt top, right side up. Smooth the layers out flat. Use white thread to baste the three layers together. Using 1″ stitches, baste a grid of vertical and horizontal lines, 3″ to 4″ apart. This grid will keep the layers together, even when you are quilting without a frame or hoop.

QUILTING

I quilt by hand with a simple running stitch. I don't use a hoop or frame. I do rock both the needle and the fabric, taking several stitches on the needle at a time. I hold the needle the same way I hold it when hand sewing a simple seam. I wear a thimble on my pushing finger (middle finger).

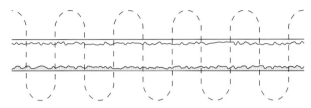

The quilting stitch

Knot a 12″ to 18″ length of hand-quilting thread. To begin stitching, pull the knot down through the quilt top into the batting and come up to the top again. This buries the knot in the batting. To end, knot the thread close to the quilt top and pull it into the batting. Let the needle travel its length through the batting and come up to the top again. Carefully snip off the thread. I like to travel the needle at a right angle to the line of quilting.

Be careful not to push or pull the layers as you quilt. Keep the work relaxed and trust the basting to hold. This will result in a nice flat quilt.

I used natural-color quilt thread throughout the projects. With these little quilts, I began by quilting the dogs. When the design allows, try to start your quilting from the center and work outward. However, where you begin quilting is not critical on small pieces like these. Normally I do not quilt through my appliqué, but these large areas of appliqué needed to be secured, both functionally and as a design element. It is a bit slow quilting through several layers, but just take one stitch at a time. I quilt around the entire outside line of the dog and then around the main appliqué pieces. This gives the dog a nice dimension.

The background and borders can be quilted as one section, so the quilt design continues right from the background out into the border, ignoring the color change. (See Corgi on page 33.) Or the background and border can be quilted as separate sections with different designs. (See Alaskan Malamute on page 22.)

DESIGN AND MARKING

Using a light, plain background fabric for your appliqué provides the perfect canvas for quilting designs. The shadows and lines created become an important part of the overall look of the quilt. The possibilities for quilting design are endless. I use random patterns, designing as I sew. I keep the markings to a minimum and the fun to the maximum. None of the designs on these dog quilts were marked prior to basting.

TIP

Use a cutting mat or a large piece of cardboard to protect your table while basting.

Basting

TIP

To audition a fabric for the border, lay the motif on top with the border fabric revealed all around. The same will help with choosing binding fabrics.

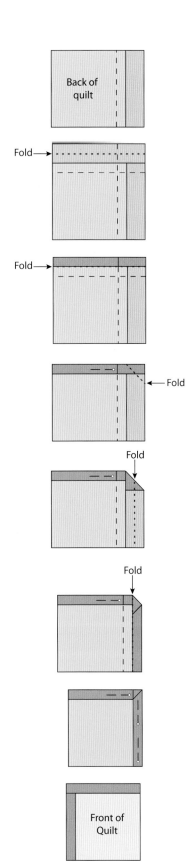

Binding (fold lines shown in red)

Straight Lines If I'm quilting parallel, crosshatched, or radiating lines, I use masking tape as a marking device. Quilt along the edge of the tape. Do not leave the tape on for more than a day. (See Poodle on page 47 and Labrador Retriever on page 42.)

Templates For repeated shapes, such as squares, circles, or triangles, cut a template from strong paper or nonwoven interfacing. Pin the template to the quilt and quilt around it. Keep moving the template around to form a unique design. On the Golden Retriever on page 39, I used a triangle and overlapped the designs. For the Bichon Frise on page 28, I used a heart shape and did not overlap the designs.

Use a blue removable marker for designs such as the large heart in the Corgi on page 33 or the hand-drawn feather used in the Labrador Retriever on page 42. Take the marks out with a damp (not dripping) paper towel.

For small designs, you can mark as you go with a blue removable marker or mark by pressing the tip of your needle into the fabric. This creates an indentation that lasts long enough to quilt, and there is nothing to remove later. I used a blue marker for the random four-petal flowers on the Scottish Terrier on page 51, and I used needle marking for the random squares around the German Boxer on page 35.

There are many ways to find inspiration for quilting designs. Try doodling designs on some paper, looking at the designs in fabrics, or drawing a secondary picture behind the appliqué. For example, see the poppies behind the Chihuahua on page 30 and the sunflower petals surrounding the Mastiff on page 45. There are designs out there waiting for you to find them.

BINDING

After the quilting is finished, remove the basting threads and any markings. Trim the batting and backing flush with the quilt top, keeping the piece square.

I use straight, single-fold, cross-grain binding. Cut the strips 2¼″ wide, selvage to selvage. Stitch the binding to the quilt using a ½″ seam. This will result in a ½″ finished bound edge. As with borders, I stitch the binding to the sides of the quilt first, then to the top and bottom. I like to stitch the binding on by hand if I have hand quilted, as it keeps the piece smoother and consistent.

Turn the binding to the back of the quilt and fold under the raw edge to meet the quilt edge and then fold again to meet the stitch line on the back of the quilt. Miter the corners following the illustrations.

I pin the entire binding in place before stitching it down. I use a blind stitch, as for the appliqué, being careful not to stitch through to the front.

Don't forget to make and attach a label to your quilt. Write a little history of the quilt and its subject to follow it through time. And, of course, sign and date the quilt.

Chapter 4:

THE KENNEL

Alaskan
Malamute

Basset Hound

Beagle

Bichon Frise

Chihuahua

Cocker Spaniel
(American)

Collie (Rough
Coated)

Corgi

Dachshund

German Boxer

German
Shepherd

Golden Retriever

Jack Russell
Terrier

Labrador
Retriever

Magyar Vizsla
(Hungarian Pointer)

Mastiff

Poodle

Pug

Scottish Terrier

Shih Tzu

West Highland
White Terrier

Yorkshire Terrier

Each of these dogs is ready for a simple portrait. Or you may want to include one or more in a larger project. The easy-to-follow instructions include the finished size of the background. Cut all backgrounds 1″ larger or more all around to allow for changes during the appliqué and the ¼″ seam allowance. The cut width of the border is listed, as well as the order of appliqué, instructions for making the eyes, pre-appliqué numbers, and any special details, if needed.

Please read the preceding chapters as well as the individual project instructions to make your piece come together smoothly.

The finished size of each piece is the actual size the quilt measures after quilting and binding.

ALASKAN MALAMUTE

Finished size: 14″ × 16¼″
Finished background: 9″ × 11¼″

Materials

🐾 **Muslin background:** ⅓ yard

🐾 Selection of fabrics for appliqué

🐾 **Border:** ¼ yard

🐾 **Binding:** ¼ yard

🐾 **Backing:** ½ yard

🐾 **Batting:** 16″ × 19″

🐾 Sewing thread to match appliqué fabrics

🐾 Natural-color quilting thread

🐾 Eye materials (refer to page 7)

Cutting

Background: Cut muslin at least 11″ × 14″.

Border: Cut 2 strips 2¾″ wide from the full width of the fabric.

Details

Eyes: Color in the dog's left eye socket with black paint prior to appliqué. Glue the dog's right eye over piece 10.

Pre-appliqué: 6 on 5; add 7; 9 on 8.

Eye patterns

> " An active dog known for pulling sleds, the Alaskan malamute loves winter, cold, and its owner. "

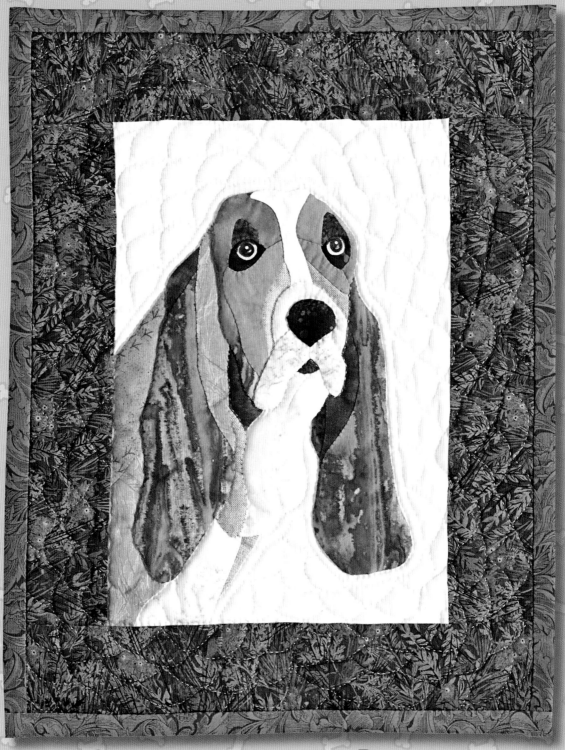

BASSET HOUND

Finished size: 13″ × 16¾″
Finished background: 8″ × 11¾″

Materials

- **Muslin background:** ⅓ yard
- Selection of fabrics for appliqué
- **Border:** ¼ yard
- **Binding:** ¼ yard
- **Backing:** ½ yard
- **Batting:** 15″ × 19″
- Sewing thread to match appliqué fabrics
- Natural-color quilting thread
- Eye materials (refer to page 7)

Cutting

Background: Cut muslin at least 10″ × 14″.

Border: Cut 2 strips 2¾″ wide from the full width of the fabric.

Details

Eyes: Color in the eye sockets with black paint prior to appliqué.

Pre-appliqué: 19 on 18; 21 on 20.

> I am not sad, only thoughtful and loving. Patience with children makes the basset hound breed a good choice for a family pet.

Eye patterns

BEAGLE

Finished size: 13¾″ × 19¼″
Finished background: 7¼″ × 12¾″

BEAGLE

Materials

- **Muslin background:** ⅓ yard
- Selection of fabrics for appliqué
- **Border:** ⅓ yard
- **Binding:** ¼ yard
- **Backing:** ½ yard
- **Batting:** 16″ × 22″
- Sewing thread to match appliqué fabrics
- Natural-color quilting thread
- Eye materials (refer to page 7)

Cutting

Background: Cut muslin at least 10″ × 15″.

Border: Cut 2 strips 3½″ wide from the full width of the fabric.

Details

Eyes: Color in the eye sockets with black paint prior to appliqué.

Pre-appliqué: 2 on 1; 3 on 4; 8 on 9; 11 on 10; 14 on 12 and 13; 16 and 17 on 15; 19 and 20 on 18.

> Dear to my heart, these friendly, playful dogs were my husband's hunting companions and part of our family for years.

Eye patterns

BICHON FRISE
Finished size: 15½˝ × 14¾˝
Finished background: 8½˝ × 7¾˝

Materials

- **Muslin background:** ⅓ yard
- Selection of fabrics for appliqué
- **Border:** ¼ yard
- **Binding:** ¼ yard
- **Backing:** ½ yard
- **Batting:** 18″ × 17″
- Sewing thread to match appliqué fabrics
- Natural-color quilting thread
- Eye materials (refer to page 7)
- Black metallic floss
- **Optional:** Silk ribbon, pendant, fabric flower

Cutting

Background: Cut muslin at least 11″ × 10″.

Border: Cut 2 strips 3¾″ wide from the full width of the fabric.

Details

Eyes: Color in the eye sockets with black paint prior to appliqué.

Feet: Add 20 and 21 after the borders. Use a black Pigma pen for the toes.

Special notes: Sew black metallic floss dots on the muzzle. Embellish as you wish after quilting. I added a stone heart pendant on two pieces of silk ribbon to the neck and a fabric flower to the border.

Eye patterns

> "Bouncy" describes these furry creatures. A good haircut makes the bichon frise beyond cute!

> With long hair or short, these little dogs are full of personality and spunk.

CHIHUAHUA

Finished size: 15½″ × 15″
Finished background: 10½″ × 10″

Materials

- 🐾 **Muslin background:** ⅓ yard
- 🐾 Selection of fabrics for appliqué
- 🐾 **Border:** ¼ yard
- 🐾 **Binding:** ¼ yard
- 🐾 **Backing:** ½ yard
- 🐾 **Batting:** 18″ × 17″
- 🐾 Sewing thread to match appliqué fabrics
- 🐾 Natural-color quilting thread
- 🐾 Eye materials (refer to page 7)

Cutting

Background: Cut muslin at least 13″ × 12″.

Border: Cut 2 strips 2¾″ wide from the full width of the fabric.

Details

Eyes: Color in the dog's right eye socket with black paint prior to appliqué. Glue the dog's left eye onto piece 17.

Pre-appliqué: 2 on 1; 9 on 8; 12 on 11.

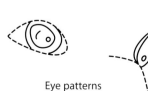

Eye patterns

> A family dog, the cocker spaniel craves human companionship.

COCKER SPANIEL
(American)

Finished size: 22½″ × 20¼″
Finished background: 16½″ × 14¼″

Materials

- **Muslin background:** ½ yard
- Selection of fabrics for appliqué
- **Border:** ⅓ yard
- **Binding:** ¼ yard
- **Backing:** ⅔ yard
- **Batting:** 25″ × 23″
- Sewing thread to match appliqué fabrics
- Natural-color quilting thread
- Eye materials (refer to page 7)

Cutting

Background: Cut muslin at least 19″ × 17″.

Border: Cut 2 strips 3¼″ wide from the full width of the fabric.

Details

Eye: Paint the eye and glue it on top of piece 11.

Pre-appliqué: 5 on 4; 18 on 17.

Eye Pattern

> "The collie, the loyal and intelligent Lassie of our child-hoods, rates high for trainability."

COLLIE (Rough Coated)

Finished size: 16¾″ × 14½″
Finished background: 11¾″ × 9½″

Materials

🐾 **Muslin background:** ⅓ yard

🐾 Selection of fabrics for appliqué

🐾 **Border:** ¼ yard

🐾 **Binding:** ¼ yard

🐾 **Backing:** ½ yard

🐾 **Batting:** 19″ × 17″

🐾 Sewing thread to match appliqué fabrics

🐾 Natural-color quilting thread

🐾 Eye materials (refer to page 7)

Cutting

Background: Cut muslin at least 14″ × 12″.

Border: Cut 2 strips 2¾″ wide from the full width of the fabric.

Details

Eye: Color in the eye socket with black paint prior to appliqué.

Mouth: Color in the mouth with black paint prior to appliqué.

Pre-appliqué: 7, 8, and 9 on 6; 11 on 10; 17, 18, and 19 on 16; 21 on 20; 23 on 22.

Eye Pattern

> Officially, it's a Welsh corgi, a dog that loves to play and to herd any group it runs across.

CORGI

Finished size: 14½" × 15¾"
Finished background: 8½" × 9¾"

Materials

🐾 **Muslin background:** ⅓ yard

🐾 Selection of fabrics for appliqué

🐾 **Border:** ¼ yard

🐾 **Binding:** ¼ yard

🐾 **Backing:** ½ yard

🐾 **Batting:** 17" × 18"

🐾 Sewing thread to match appliqué fabrics

🐾 Natural-color quilting thread

🐾 Eye materials (refer to page 7)

Cutting

Background: Cut muslin at least 11" × 12".

Border: Cut 2 strips 3¼" wide from the full width of the fabric.

Details

Eyes: Color in the eye sockets with black paint prior to appliqué.

Pre-appliqué: 2 on 1; 7 on 6; 11 on 10; 14 on 13.

Eye patterns

DACHSHUND

Finished size: 20¼″ × 13½″
Finished background: 15¼″ × 8½″

Materials

- 🐾 **Muslin background:** ⅓ yard
- 🐾 Selection of fabrics for appliqué
- 🐾 **Border:** ¼ yard
- 🐾 **Binding:** ¼ yard
- 🐾 **Backing:** ½ yard
- 🐾 **Batting:** 23″ × 16″
- 🐾 Sewing thread to match appliqué fabrics
- 🐾 Natural-color quilting thread
- 🐾 Eye materials (refer to page 7)

Cutting

Background: Cut muslin at least 18″ × 11″.

Border: Cut 2 strips 2¾″ wide from the full width of the fabric.

Details

Eye: Color in the eye socket with black paint prior to appliqué.

Pre-appliqué: 9 on 8; 15 on 14; 19 on 18.

Eye Pattern

> " Good watchdogs, dachshunds come in three sizes and in three hair types: standard, miniature, or toy and short hair, wirehair, or longhair. "

German Boxer

Finished size: 20½˝ × 18¼˝
Finished background: 15½˝ × 13¼˝

GERMAN BOXER

Materials

- **Muslin background:** ½ yard
- Selection of fabrics for appliqué
- **Border:** ¼ yard
- **Binding:** ¼ yard
- **Backing:** ⅝ yard
- **Batting:** 23″ × 21″
- Sewing thread to match appliqué fabrics
- Natural-color quilting thread
- Eye materials (refer to page 7)

Cutting

Background: Cut muslin at least 18″ × 16″.

Border: Cut 2 strips 2¾″ wide from the full width of the fabric.

Details

Eye: Paint the eye and glue it on top of piece 27.

Pre-appliqué: 4 on 3; 6 on 5; 11 on 10; 12 on 11; 30 on 29.

Eye Pattern

> Great defenders yet patient with children, German boxers are fine pets that enjoy sports.

German Shepherd

Finished size: 16½″ × 17½″
Finished background: 11½″ × 12½″

Materials

🐾 **Muslin background:** ½ yard

🐾 Selection of fabrics for appliqué

🐾 **Border:** ¼ yard

🐾 **Binding:** ¼ yard

🐾 **Backing:** ⅝ yard

🐾 **Batting:** 19″ × 20″

🐾 Sewing thread to match appliqué fabrics

🐾 Natural-color quilting thread

🐾 Eye materials (refer to page 7)

Cutting

Background: Cut muslin at least 14″ × 15″.

Border: Cut 2 strips 2¾″ wide from the full width of the fabric.

Details

Eye: Color in the eye socket with black paint prior to appliqué.

Mouth: Color in the mouth area with black paint prior to appliqué.

Pre-appliqué: 7 on 6; 13 and 12 on 11.

" The German shepherd
is the best breed
for guiding the blind,
helping the handicapped,
rescuing people, and
assisting the police. "

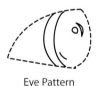

Eye Pattern

Materials

🐾 **Muslin background:** ⅓ yard

🐾 Selection of fabrics for appliqué

🐾 **Border:** ⅓ yard

🐾 **Binding:** ¼ yard

🐾 **Backing:** ⅝ yard

🐾 **Batting:** 19″ × 29″

🐾 Sewing thread to match appliqué fabrics

🐾 Natural-color quilting thread

🐾 Eye materials (refer to page 7)

Cutting

Background: Cut muslin at least 12″ × 22″.

Border: Cut 2 strips 4″ wide from the full width of the fabric.

Details

Eyes: Color in the eye sockets with black paint prior to appliqué.

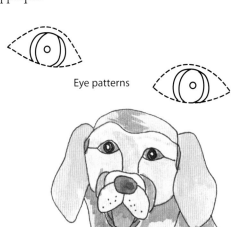

Eye patterns

GOLDEN RETRIEVER

Finished size: 17″ × 27″
Finished background: 9½″ × 19½″

> This is a dog for the entire family. Golden retrievers love to swim and, of course, retrieve.

JACK RUSSELL TERRIER

Finished size: 18˝ × 19½˝
Finished background: 12˝ × 13½˝

Materials

- **Muslin background:** ½ yard

- Selection of fabrics for appliqué

- **Border:** ⅓ yard

- **Binding:** ¼ yard

- **Backing:** ⅝ yard

- **Batting:** 20″ × 22″

- Sewing thread to match appliqué fabrics

- Natural-color quilting thread

- Eye materials (refer to page 7)

- Brown embroidery floss

> Possessing a mind of its own, this independent little dog needs plenty of attention and activity.

Cutting

Background: Cut muslin at least 14″ × 16″.

Border: Cut 2 strips 3¼″ wide from the full width of the fabric.

Details

Eyes: Color in the eye sockets with black paint prior to appliqué.

Ears: Construct the ears according to the instructions on page 15. Insert the ears (12 and 12 reversed) under 13 and 14 with right side down. Fold the ears down to reflect your favorite expression.

Pre-appliqué: 2 on 1; 9 on 8; 17 on 16; 19 on 18; 24 on 22 and 23.

Special notes: Make the muzzle dots with a black Pigma pen. After quilting, stem stitch around the dog in brown floss.

Eye patterns

LABRADOR RETRIEVER
Finished size: 25″ × 29½″
Finished background: 15″ × 19½″

Materials

- **Muslin background:** ½ yard
- Selection of fabrics for appliqué
- **Inner border:** ⅛ yard
- **Outer border:** ½ yard
- **Binding:** ¼ yard
- **Backing:** ⅞ yard
- **Batting:** 27″ × 32″
- Sewing thread to match appliqué fabrics
- Natural-color quilting thread
- Eye materials (refer to page 7)

> Good hunting dogs, Labrador retrievers like to play. They have good tempers and are friendly, which makes them just super dogs all around!

Cutting

Background: Cut muslin at least 17″ × 22″.

Inner border: Cut 2 strips 1¼″ wide from the full width of the fabric.

Outer border: Cut 3 strips 4½″ wide from the full width of the fabric.

Details

Eye: Color in the eye socket with black paint prior to appliqué.

Pre-appliqué: 16 on 15; 34 on 33.

Special notes: Pieces 1–9 are for the bench. Piping may be added between pieces 8 and 9.

Eye Pattern

> Also called a Hungarian pointer, the Magyar Vizsla is a talented hunting dog and a fine companion. I am acquainted with one named Bailey."

MAGYAR VIZSLA
(Hungarian Pointer)
Finished size: 16½″ × 14″
Finished background: 11½″ × 9″

Materials

🐾 **Muslin background:** ⅓ yard

🐾 Selection of fabrics for appliqué

🐾 **Border:** ¼ yard

🐾 **Binding:** ¼ yard

🐾 **Backing:** ½ yard

🐾 **Batting:** 19″ × 16″

🐾 Sewing thread to match appliqué fabrics

🐾 Natural-color quilting thread

🐾 Eye materials (refer to page 7)

Cutting

Background: Cut muslin at least 14″ × 11″.

Border: Cut 2 strips 2¾″ wide from the full width of the fabric.

Details

Eyes: Color in the eye sockets on the background piece with rusty-colored paint to match the fur color prior to appliqué.

Eye patterns

MASTIFF

Finished size: 17½″ × 18¼″
Finished background: 10″ × 10¾″

Materials

- **Muslin background:** ⅓ yard
- Selection of fabrics for appliqué
- **Border:** ⅓ yard
- **Binding:** ¼ yard
- **Backing:** ⅔ yard
- **Batting:** 20″ × 21″
- Sewing thread to match appliqué fabrics
- Natural-color quilting thread
- Eye materials (refer to page 7)

Cutting

Background: Cut muslin at least 12″ × 13″.

Border: Cut 2 strips 4″ wide from the full width of the fabric.

Details

Eyes: Color in the eye sockets with black paint prior to appliqué.

Nose and mouth: Color in the nostrils and mouth with black paint prior to appliqué.

Pre-appliqué: 13 on 12; add 14 and set aside; 17 on 16, then on 15, and then all 3 to background; then add the 12, 13, 14 set; 19 on 18, add 20, and set aside; 23 on 22, then on 21, and then all 3 to the background; add the 19, 18, 20 set.

Eye patterns

> Big, noble, and gentle, the mastiff is an ancient breed that's full of love.

POODLE
Finished size: 18½″ × 23¼″
Finished background: 10½″ × 15¼″

Materials

- **Muslin background:** ⅜ yard
- Selection of fabrics for appliqué
- **Border:** ⅜ yard
- **Binding:** ¼ yard
- **Backing:** ⅝ yard
- **Batting:** 21″ × 26″
- Sewing thread to match appliqué fabrics
- Natural-color quilting thread
- Eye materials (refer to page 7)

Cutting

Background: Cut muslin at least 13″ × 18″.

Border: Cut 2 strips 4¼″ wide from the full width of the fabric.

Details

Eyes: Color in the eye sockets with black paint prior to appliqué.

Ears: Construct the ears according to the instructions on page 15. Insert the ears as pieces 9a and 9b.

> Small, medium, or large, these intelligent dogs make great pets. Poodles are excellent indoor dogs.

Eye patterns

PUG

Finished size: 18½″ × 20½″
Finished background: 11″ × 13″

PUG

Materials

- **Muslin background:** ⅜ yard
- Selection of fabrics for appliqué
- **Border:** ⅓ yard
- **Binding:** ¼ yard
- **Backing:** ⅝ yard
- **Batting:** 21″ × 23″
- Sewing thread to match appliqué fabrics
- Natural-color quilting thread
- Eye materials (refer to page 7)

Cutting

Background: Cut muslin at least 13″ × 15″.

Border: Cut 2 strips 4″ wide from the full width of the fabric.

Details

Eyes: Color in the eye sockets with black paint prior to appliqué.

Mouth: Color in the mouth with black paint prior to appliqué.

Toes: Mark the toes with a black Pigma pen.

Ears: Construct the ears according to the instructions on page 15. Insert as pieces 28 and 28 reversed. Fold the ears down to reflect your favorite expression.

Pre-appliqué: 31 on 30; 33 on 32.

Eye patterns

> Friendly little fellows that are easy to train, pugs are happy house pets.

SCOTTISH TERRIER

Finished size: 20¼″ × 17¾″
Finished background: 13¼″ × 10¾″

Scottish Terrier

Materials

- **Muslin background:** ⅜ yard
- Selection of fabrics for appliqué
- **Border:** ⅓ yard
- **Binding:** ¼ yard
- **Backing:** ⅝ yard
- **Batting:** 23″ × 20″
- Sewing thread to match appliqué fabrics
- Natural-color quilting thread
- Eye materials (refer to page 7)

Cutting

Background: Cut muslin at least 16″ × 13″.

Border: Cut 2 strips 3¾″ wide from the full width of the fabric.

Details

Eye: Color in the eye socket with black paint prior to appliqué.

Pre-appliqué: 9 on 8; 12 on 13, then on 11; 19 on 18.

Eye Pattern

> I need lots of exercise and I won't always obey—but aren't I something?

Shih Tzu

Finished size: 17¼″ × 18½″
Finished background: 10¾″ × 12″

Materials

- **Muslin background:** ⅜ yard
- Selection of fabrics for appliqué
- **Border:** ⅓ yard
- **Binding:** ¼ yard
- **Backing:** ⅝ yard
- **Batting:** 20″ × 21″
- Sewing thread to match appliqué fabrics
- Natural-color quilting thread
- Eye materials (refer to page 7)

Cutting

Background: Cut muslin at least 13″ × 14″.

Border: Cut 2 strips 3½″ wide from the full width of the fabric.

Details

Eyes: Color in the eye sockets with black paint prior to appliqué.

Pre-appliqué: 2 on 1.

> The lion dog, the shih tzu needs lots of grooming, unless it gets a haircut. The shih tzu loves to be loved, and loves in return.

Eye patterns

WEST HIGHLAND WHITE TERRIER

Finished size: 16¾″ × 14½″
Finished background: 11¾″ × 9½″

WEST HIGHLAND WHITE TERRIER

Materials

- **Muslin background:** ⅓ yard
- Selection of fabrics for appliqué
- **Border:** ¼ yard
- **Binding:** ¼ yard
- **Backing:** ½ yard
- **Batting:** 19″ × 17″
- Sewing thread to match appliqué fabrics
- Natural-color quilting thread
- Eye materials (refer to page 7)
- Brown embroidery floss

> The Westie is a pure white character with a special charm.

Cutting

Background: Cut muslin at least 14″ × 12″.

Border: Cut 2 strips 2¾″ wide from the full width of the fabric.

Details

Eye: Color in the eye socket with black paint prior to appliqué.

Pre-appliqué: 15 on 14; 23 and 22 on 21.

Special note: After quilting, stem stitch around the dog using brown floss.

Eye Pattern

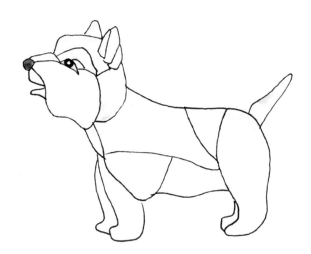

YORKSHIRE TERRIER

Finished size: 13½″ × 17¼″
Finished background: 7½″ × 11¼″

Materials

- **Muslin background:** ⅓ yard
- Selection of fabrics for appliqué
- **Border:** ⅓ yard
- **Binding:** ¼ yard
- **Backing:** ½ yard
- **Batting:** 16″ × 20″
- Sewing thread to match appliqué fabrics
- Natural-color quilting thread
- Eye materials (refer to page 7)

Cutting

Background: Cut muslin at least 10″ × 14″.

Border: Cut 2 strips 3¼″ wide from the full width of the fabric.

Details

Eyes: Color in the eye sockets with black paint prior to appliqué.

Pre-appliqué: 13 on 12; 15 on 14.

Eye patterns

> Yorkshire terriers are so tiny, but they don't know it. They will chase even the biggest of dogs.

BLUE EYES
Finished size: 13″ × 17″

Materials

🐾 **Mottled fabric for dog:** 7½″ × 10″

🐾 Assorted blue scraps for frame

🐾 **Muslin background:** 10″ × 13″

🐾 **Backing:** 15″ × 19″

🐾 **Batting:** 15″ × 19″

🐾 **Paper-backed fusible web:** 7½″ × 10″

Construction

1. Iron fusible web to the wrong side of the dog fabric, following the manufacturer's instructions.

2. Trace the dog of your choice on the right side of the fused fabric. (I selected an abbreviated version of the Golden Retriever, page 39.) Trace interior lines as well as outer shape.

3. Cut out the dog as one piece. Fuse it to the center of the background fabric.

4. Place the backing wrong side up and layer the batting on top. Center the background right side up on the batting. Use a few pins to hold it in place.

Let the fabric do the work. This quick fused and machine-stitched fellow makes good use of marbled fabric.

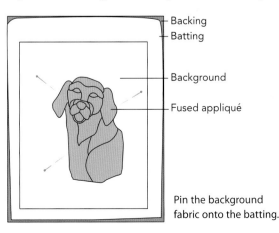

Backing
Batting

Background

Fused appliqué

Pin the background fabric onto the batting.

5. "Draw" over all the marked lines with machine stitching in a contrasting color. Use free-motion or standard stitching. This is a place to play! I went over the lines several times to give the piece the look of a sketch.

Outline the dog with stitching.

6. Paint the eyes directly onto the dog (page 16). I also added some pink paint to the tongue and a few black dots on the muzzle. Allow the paint to dry completely.

7. Using blue scraps, sew and flip pieces around the central motif, pressing each piece flat as you go. Refer to the photo on page 59 for the approximate size and position of the pieces for the frame.

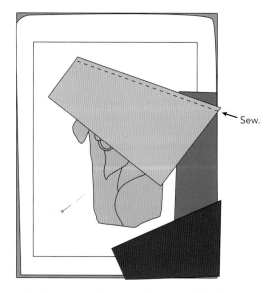

Add strips around the center block to build a frame.

8. Press the finished piece and trim it to approximately 13″ × 17″.

9. There is no binding for this little work; it is raw edged. Run 3 parallel rows of machine stitches close together around the outer edge. Use a rotary cutter to trim any batting that shows.

It's quick, it's fun, and it's a great opportunity to play with new machine techniques!

BUTTONS
Finished size: 18″ × 24¾″

Materials

- 🐾 **Muslin background:** 11″ × 11″

- 🐾 Selection of dog fabrics for appliqué

- 🐾 **Light fabric:** 19 squares, 2¾″ × 2¾″

- 🐾 **Assorted dark fabrics:** 19 squares, 2¾″ × 2¾″

- 🐾 **Border:** ¼ yard

- 🐾 19 assorted buttons, ¾″ to 1″ in diameter

- 🐾 **Backing:** 20″ × 27″

- 🐾 **Batting:** 20″ × 27″

- 🐾 **Paper-backed fusible web:** 10″ × 10″

Cutting

Border: Cut 2 strips 3″ wide from the full width of the fabric.

Construction

1. Trace the reverse of all the appliqué pieces on the paper backing of the fusible web. (I chose the Yorkie on page 58.) Cut out each piece with a ⅛″ allowance and fuse each piece to the back of the appropriate appliqué fabric, following the manufacturer's instructions. Vary the colors to differentiate between adjacent pieces.

2. Cut each appliqué piece to the exact size and put all the pieces together, like a puzzle, on the background fabric. Use a light pencil to draw the dog onto the background fabric as a placement guide, if necessary.

3. Fuse the pieces in place.

4. Machine stitch around each piece with a narrow, dense zigzag stitch in a dark color. (I used black, and I also added some stitching to the dog's ear.)

5. Make the eyes (see page 16) and glue them in place. Trim the appliquéd block to 9½″ × 9½″.

6. Use the 2¾″ squares to sew a block 4 squares wide by 5 squares long. Sew a strip 2 squares wide by 9 squares long. Refer to the photo for placement. Use a ¼″ seam.

7. Sew the appliquéd block to the 4 × 5 pieced block. Add the pieced strip to the left side. Press well.

He's just as cute as a button! This fun project will show off some of those buttons you've been saving. I used fusible appliqué for this piece. Any of the appliqué dogs can be used—just adjust the size of the dog to fit the quilt or the size of the quilt to fit the dog!

8. Measure the length of the quilt and cut 2 borders to this length. Sew to the sides of the quilt. Press.

9. Measure the width of the quilt, including the borders just added, and cut 2 borders to this length. Sew to the top and bottom of the quilt.

10. Layer the batting, then the backing right side up, then the finished top right side down. Stitch all around with a ½″ seam allowance, leaving a 4″ opening on one side. Trim the seam allowance to ¼″ and cut the corners to 45°. Turn the piece right side out. Smooth out the edges and corners and press flat. Close the opening with a bit of fusible web.

11. Quilt as you like. I quilted by hand with a simple line diagonally through the squares in both directions and around the dog. Quilt about ¼″ from the outer edge to simulate binding.

12. Stitch a button in the center of each light square, being sure to sew through all 3 quilt layers to secure them.

Postscript

If you have not found your dog here, nominations are being accepted
for a possible sequel!

ABOUT THE AUTHOR

Carol gives dogs their day with this latest book. Country life goes hand in hand with canine companions. Carol and her cabinetmaker husband enjoy a creative homestead life in Michigan's Upper Peninsula, where the long, snowy winters give her lots of time for creating and quilting.

Since teaching herself to quilt in 1980, Carol has developed her own artistic style, but she credits nature for being an unending source of ideas. Developing these ideas is not all that occupies her time, however. When she needs a break from her creative pursuits, there is water to pump and bring into the house, wood to load in the wood box, bird feeders to fill, and a large organic vegetable garden to tend.

Also by Carol Armstrong

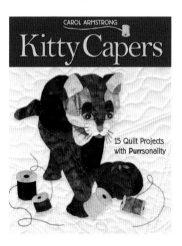

For a list of other fine books from C&T Publishing, ask for a free catalog:

C&T Publishing, Inc.
P.O. Box 1456
Lafayette, CA 94549
(800) 284-1114
Email: ctinfo@ctpub.com
Website: www.ctpub.com

C&T Publishing's professional photography services are now available to the public. Visit us at www.ctmediaservices.com.

For quilting supplies:

Cotton Patch
1025 Brown Ave.
Lafayette, CA 94549
Store: (925) 284-1177
Mail order: (925) 283-7883
Email: CottonPa@aol.com
Website: www.quiltusa.com

Note

Fabrics used in the projects shown may not be currently available, as fabric manufacturers keep most fabrics in print for only a short time.

Great Titles

from

C&T PUBLISHING